KT-464-477

Books should be returned on or before the
last date stamped below

1 6 DEC 2002

2 8 FEB 2004

1 6 APR 2004

1 4 MAY 2004

- 8 OCT 2004

2 1 JUL 2004

HQ

2 3 SEP 2008

- 9 SEP 2010

1 2 MAR 2011

2 9 MAY 2012

2 6 JUN 2012

1 4 DEC 2013

1 9 MAR 2016

3 0 JUN 2018

ABERDEENSHIRE LIBRARY
AND INFORMATION SERVICE
MELDRUM MEG WAY, OLDMELDRUM

Powell,Jillian

From calf to cow

A L I S

1203314

ABERDEENSHIRE LIBRARY & INFORMATION SERVICE		
12 03314		
CBS	09/08/2002	
J636.2	9.99	
JNF	OLDP	PD

How Do They Grow?

From Calf to Cow

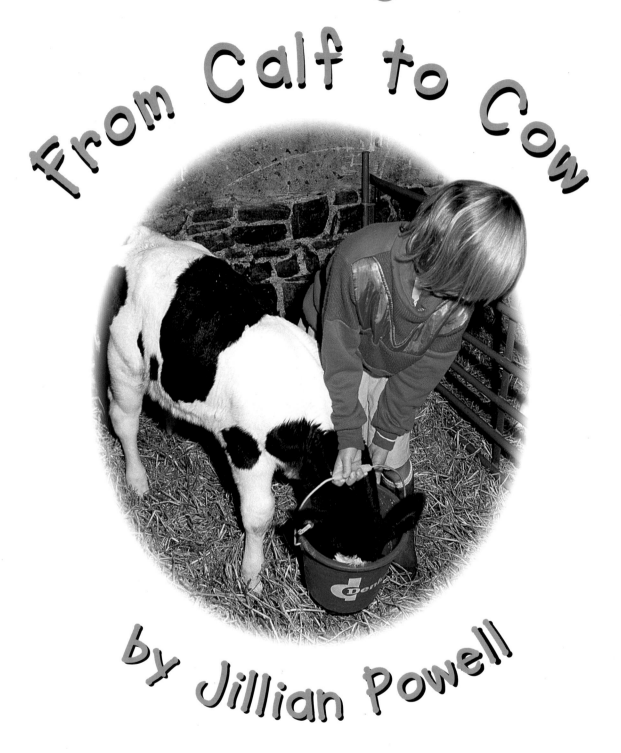

by Jillian Powell

HODDER
Wayland

an imprint of Hodder Children's Books

© 2001 White-Thomson Publishing Ltd

Produced for Hodder Wayland by
White-Thomson Publishing Ltd
2/3 St. Andrew's Place
Lewes, East Sussex
BN7 1UP

Editor: Sarah Doughty
Designer: Tessa Barwick
Text consultant: Jessica Buss
Language consultant: Norah Granger

Published in Great Britain in 2001 by Hodder Wayland,
an imprint of Hodder Children's Books.

The right of Jillian Powell to be identified as the author has been asserted by her in accordance
with the Copyright, Designs and Patents Act 1998.

All rights reserved. No part of this publication may be reproduced, stored in a retrieval system,
or transmitted, in any form or by any means without the prior written permission of the
publisher, nor be otherwise circulated in any form of binding or cover other than that in which it
is published and without a similar condition being imposed on the subsequent purchaser.

British Library Cataloguing in Publication Data
    Powell, Jillian
        From calf to cow. – (How do they grow?)
        1. Calves – Development – Juvenile literature 2. Cows –
        Physiology – Juvenile literature
        I. Title
        636.2

ISBN 0 7502 2732 X

Printed and bound in Italy by G.Canale & C.S.p.A.

Hodder Children's Books
A division of Hodder Headline Ltd
338 Euston Road, London NW1 3BH

Contents

Words in **bold** in the text can be found in the glossary on page 30.

Giving birth

This **cow** will soon give birth to a calf. The calf has been growing inside her for nearly nine months.

A calf has just been born. It can see and hear but it cannot stand up yet. The cow licks her calf to dry and clean it.

The newborn

dairy calf

The newborn calf is soon standing on its feet.

Its legs are weak and wobbly at first.

Its coat is still damp.

A calf starts to drink its mother's milk. Her milk will protect the calf against **germs** and **diseases**.

Feeding the calves

Dairy calves are taken away from their mothers after a few days. This stops them drinking all the cows' milk. The farmer sells this milk to people.

The dairy calves are now fed a milk drink made from dried milk mixed with water. They drink their milk from buckets.

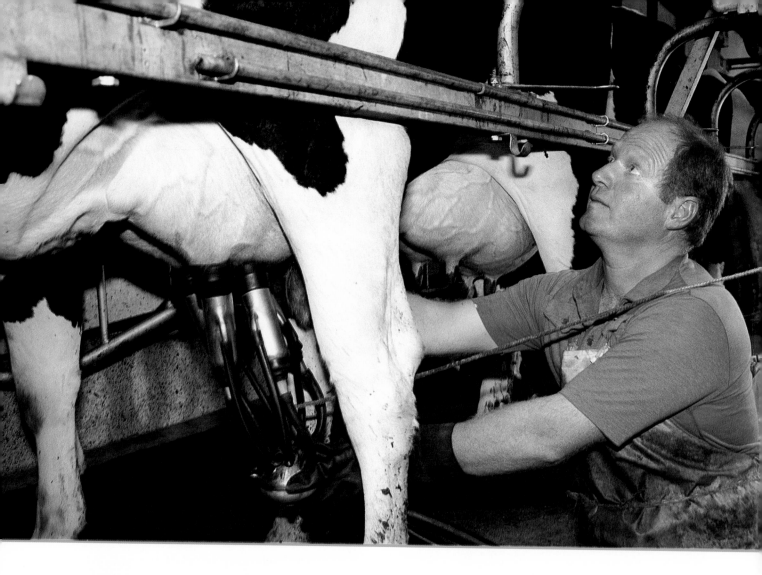

Dairy cows give milk

When a dairy cow has given birth to a calf, she can be milked for about ten months. Cows are milked twice a day to provide milk for people to drink.

The cows can eat while they are being milked. Each dairy cow has a number on her back so the farmer can tell which cows give the most milk.

Looking after the calves

A vet visits the farm to check that this calf is healthy. Calves will be given **medicine** if they are sick.

Young calves have
their horns taken off.
This is so they
cannot hurt
themselves
or each
other.

Beef calves

Calves which are born on a beef farm stay with their mothers. The young calves drink their mothers' milk until they are about six months old.

14

Some beef calves are kept indoors all year round. Others go out into the fields in the spring where they can **graze** on the grass with the cows.

Young calves

These dairy calves are about eight weeks old.
They live together in a straw pen. The farmer
starts to give them solid food to eat
from a **trough**.

Each calf has a **tag** in each ear. The tags help the farmer tell the calves apart.

Indoor feeding

This dairy calf likes nibbling **hay** from a hay rack. The farmer feeds the calves hay or **silage** in the winter.

The calves also eat dry food made from a mixture of **grains** and beans. This helps them to grow fast. They drink plenty of water every day too.

Spring grazing

In the spring, there is plenty of fresh grass in the fields. Dairy calves which were born in the autumn can now go outside. They can graze on the grass.

Cows and calves eat lots of grass. A cow can eat as much as 70 kg of grass in a day. The grass feeds her and helps her to make lots of milk.

Growing up in

the fields

These beef calves like to play together out in the fields. They swish their tails to keep flies away. They grow bigger and stronger.

This beef calf is growing fast. It can put on half a kilogram of weight in a day.

The beef calves are sold

When the beef calves are about a year old, they are ready to go to market. When they were born, they weighed about 45 kg. Now they weigh about 300 kg.

The calves are sold at a cattle market. Some will go to farms where they will grow for another year. When they are two years old, they are sold for beef.

Bulls and heifers

The farmer keeps a **bull** to **mate** with the **heifers** so more calves are born each year. After they have mated, some of the heifers will have calves growing inside them.

Young heifers are ready to mate when they are about sixteen months old. When these heifers have had their first calf, they will join the dairy **herd** for milking.

Having calves

This cow has mated with a bull and is **pregnant**.
On most farms, some of the calves are born in
the autumn and others are born in the spring.

This dairy cow has had her calf. It will grow up
to be as strong and healthy as she is.

Glossary

Bull An adult male in the cattle family. A bull can be the father of calves.

Cow The name given to an adult female in the cattle family, after the birth of her second calf.

Diseases Illnesses.

Germs Tiny particles around us that can carry disease.

Grains The seeds of a cereal crop.

Graze To feed on grass.

Hay Dried grass.

Heifers The name given to female cattle before they have had their second calf.

Herd A group of cattle.

Mate When a male and female have come together to have babies. A male gives a female a seed which makes a female egg grow into a baby animal.

Medicine Drugs that are taken to stop illness or disease.

Pregnant When a female has young growing inside her.

Silage Stored grass that is used to feed cattle in winter.

Tag A label that shows the name or number of something.

Trough A long container that holds food or water for farm animals.

Further information

Books

A First Look at Animals on the Farm by James, Lynn and Dodds (Two Can Publishing, 2000)

Animals on the Farm by Sally Morgan (Franklin Watts, 1999)

Beef Farm and *Dairy Farm* (Let's Visit series) by Sarah Doughty & Diana Bentley (Hodder Wayland, 1989)

Farm Animals (Eye Openers series, Dorling Kindersley, 1999)

Farm Animals: Cows by Rachael Bell (Heinemann, 2000)

On the Farms by Alistair Smith (Usborne, 1999)

Who am I? Heavy and Hoofed (Cow) by Moira Butterfield (Belitha, 2000)

Video

Farm Animals narrated by Johnny Morris (Dorling Kindersley)

On the Farm: Baby Animals (Dorling Kindersley)

Let's Go to the Farm/Baby Animals (Countryside Products). Visit their website at: **www.countrysidevideos.com**

Websites

www.bbc.co.uk/education/schools
BBC education online provides lots of information about animals.

www.kidsfarm.com
A fun site about the people and animals on ranches in Colorado, USA.

www.mda.state.mi.us/kids/pictures/dairy
Pictures and facts about dairy cows and calves.

Useful addresses

The National Association of Farms for Schools provides an annual directory of farms providing facilities for school visits, and an information line. To find out more write to 164, Shaftesbury Avenue, London WC2H 8HL (tel: 01422 882 708), or visit their website at: **www.farmsforschools.org.uk**

The Food and Farming Education Service provides a directory of learning resources for primary and secondary schools and a list of local resource centres. To find out more write to Stoneleigh Park, Warwickshire, CV8 2LZ (tel: 02476 535 707), or visit their website at: **www.foodandfarming.org**

Index

Picture acknowledgements

Agripicture (Peter Dean) 8, 9, 10, 11, 14, 16, 17, 19, 20, 22, 23, 25, 26, 27; Chris Fairclough 4, 6, 12, 18, 24, 28; HWPL title page, 7, 29; NHPA 5 (Mirko Stelzner); Oxford Scientific Films 13 (Raymond Blythe); 15 (Ian West), 21 (Animals Animals/Lynn Stone).